The FBI and Cyber Crime

By Robert Grayson

MASON CREST PUBLISHERS

Produced in association with Water Buffalo Books.
Design by Westgraphix LLC.

MASON CREST PUBLISHERS INC.
370 Reed Road
Broomall, Pennsylvania 19008
(866) MCP-BOOK (toll free)
www.masoncrest.com

Printed in the United States of America

First Printing

9 8 7 6 5 4 3 2 1

Library of Congress Cataloging-in-Publication Data

Grayson, Robert, 1951-
        The FBI and cyber crimes / Robert Grayson.
            p. cm. — (The FBI story)
        Includes bibliographical references and index.
        ISBN 978-1-4222-0568-6 (hardcover : alk. paper) — ISBN 978-1-4222-1370-4 (pbk. : alk. paper)
        1. United States. Federal Bureau of Investigation—Juvenile literature. 2. Computer crimes—
United States—Juvenile literature. 3. Computer crimes—Investigation—United States—Juvenile
literature. I. Title.
        HV8079.C65G76 2009
        363.25'9680973—dc22   2008048096

Photo credits: © AP/Wide World Photos: 14, 17, 19, 28, 41; © CORBIS: 35; © Courtesy of
FBI: cover (lower left, center, lower right), 1, 4 (both), 8 (all), 9 (both), 10, 13, 20, 23, 24, 25
(upper), 26, 31, 32, 45, 47, 53, 55, 57, 62; © iStock Photos: 22; Used under license from
Shutterstock Inc.: cover (upper left, upper right), 5, 7, 25 (lower), 42, 56.

Publisher's note:
All quotations in this book come from original sources and contain the spelling and grammatical
inconsistencies of the original text.

CONTENTS

CHAPTER 1 Criminals Go High Tech

When we think of the weapons that people typically use to commit a crime, the usual assortment comes to mind: guns, knives, machetes, bombs, even fists. One weapon that usually does not spring to mind is the computer, but today, for many crooks, computers are the weapons of choice. **Cyber crime** is everywhere, and cyber criminals can live anywhere.

Criminals no longer have to battle a hail of bullets as they make their getaway in a speeding vehicle. No clever disguises are needed, no gloves to eliminate fingerprints, no waiting until dark when it is less likely they will be seen, no time spent "casing" the scene of the crime. Cyber crimes

These photos, both taken in the early 1960s, show a bank robbery in progress in "real time" (left), with robbers brandishing firearms, terrified customers and workers fearing for their lives, and a briefcase filled with explosives used to blow open a vault (right).

can be committed by one person or whole "rings" of people; they can be simple or sophisticated; and they can go on for hours or years.

From the comfort of their own homes, cyber criminals can launch a crime spree, **hackers** can steal valuable corporate secrets, **predators** can stalk children, and terrorists can **wreak havoc**, all with the push of a button. Cyber crime goes on 24 hours a day, seven days a week, all around the globe. One line of defense against those who turn modern technology on law-abiding citizens is the Federal Bureau of Investigation (FBI).

FAST FACTS

What is today known as the Federal Bureau of Investigation, or FBI, was officially founded as the Bureau of Investigation on July 26, 1908. It now serves as the investigative arm of the U.S. Department of Justice.

The cyber version of a bank robbery might originate with a hacker sitting thousands of miles from the bank. Working with a laptop instead of a briefcase filled with explosives, the hacker might use electronically stolen codes and passwords to illegally transfer millions of dollars from one account into another.

Battle in Cyberspace

In the United States, government, national defense, educational institutions, and private businesses and industries rely heavily on the information and communication that occur through computer networks. Taken as a whole, the information that is communicated through vast computer networks is known as *cyberspace*. An attack on the **infrastructure** of information technology that powers cyberspace could be devastating to a nation. In February 2003, President George W. Bush established the National Strategy to Secure Cyberspace, the framework to battle cyber crime and protect cyberspace.

In a statement about the National Strategy to Secure Cyberspace, President Bush said,

> We must act to reduce our vulnerabilities to these threats before they can be exploited to damage the cyber systems supporting our nation's critical infrastructures and ensure that such disruptions of cyberspace are infrequent, of minimal duration, manageable, and cause the least damage possible. . . . Securing cyberspace is an extraordinarily difficult strategic challenge that requires a coordinated and focused effort from our entire society—the federal government, state and local governments, the private sector, and the American people.

Growing Fast

Cyber crime is growing at an alarming rate, making it difficult for law enforcement officials—not only in the United

States but all over the world—to keep up with it. The speed with which cyber crime can be carried out makes it especially dangerous, and cyber criminals can often operate with complete **anonymity**.

Just think about the vast range of important services that government on all levels carries out: public health, social welfare, water, sewer, education, public information, finance, transportation, police, fire, and ambulance. These services now rely fully or in part on the computer infrastructure to operate at maximum efficiency. All of them could be affected by an attack by cyber criminals who either seek to disrupt those services or steal information from government databases.

FAST FACTS

As of right now, the average 21-year-old has sent and received about 250,000 emails and text messages in his or her lifetime, according to the FBI.

Both these children share the benefits of using computers for work and play. According to FBI statistics, however, as a male the boy is more likely to lose money to computer **fraud** when he grows up than is the girl. He is also—again as a male—three times more likely to commit a crime online.

In addition, private businesses use cyberspace to conduct day-to-day operations. Those businesses also need the protection of the FBI from criminal cyber attacks. It is no wonder that the FBI considers battling cyber crime to be such a high priority and has created an entire unit—the FBI Cyber Division—to deal with it.

Partnerships to Combat Cyber Crime

The FBI has partnered with various organizations to analyze and fight cyber crime as well as get the latest information about computer-related crimes out to the public. One of those partnerships—with the National White Collar Crime Center and the Bureau of Justice Assistance (like the FBI, a part of the U.S. Department of Justice)—resulted in the creation of the Internet Crime Complaint Center (IC3).

INTERNET CRIME COMPLAINT CENTER
... an FBI - NW3C Partnership

NW3C
INTEGRITY QUALITY SERVICE
National White Collar Crime Center

BJA Bureau of Justice Assistance
Solutions for Safer Communities

The Internet Crime Complaint Center, or IC3, is a super cyber crime-fighting clearinghouse. It directs complaints and information concerning cyber crime to the FBI and the other agencies, represented here by their logos, that have united to form the IC3.

The IC3 is a clearinghouse for cyber complaints from industry and private citizens alike. The information gathered by the IC3 gives the FBI, as well as other law enforcement officials on the local, state, federal, and international levels, vital information about the latest trends in computer crime. The IC3 also turns over many of the complaints it gets to law enforcement officials for investigation and prosecution.

FAST FACTS

The FBI's Cyber Division is often called in to consult on cases other FBI divisions are handling, when aggressive technological investigative help is needed.

This IC3 safety poster (right), produced by the FBI and IC3, helps ordinary computer users be on the lookout for scams and other cyber crimes on their home computers. The "Scam Email Alert" link (below) leads readers to examples of fraudulent emails to which they should never reply. Both the safety poster and the scam-email link may be viewed on the IC3 home page at http://www.ic3.gov/default.aspx.

SCAM EMAIL ALERT!

INTERNET SAFETY ALERT
FBI
INTERNET CRIME COMPLAINT CENTER
ARE YOU A SAFE INTERNET USER?
YOU MAY BE AT RISK
IF YOU ANSWER "YES" TO ANY
OF THE FOLLOWING QUESTIONS:

➤ Do you visit websites by clicking on links within an email?

➤ Do you reply to emails from companies or persons you are not familiar with?

➤ Have you received packages to hold or ship to someone you met on the Internet?

➤ Have you been asked to cash checks and wire funds to an employer you met online?

➤ Would you cash checks or money orders received through an online transaction without first confirming their legitimacy?

➤ Would you provide your personal/banking information as a result of an email notification?

DON'T BE AN INTERNET CRIME VICTIM!

FOR MORE INFORMATION AND
TO TEST YOUR ONLINE PRACTICES

The IC3 publishes an annual Internet crime report, detailing criminal activity in cyberspace over the past year. Complaints roll in daily, as Internet criminals constantly come up with new ways of using the latest computer technology to commit crimes. "The Internet presents a wealth of opportunity for would-be criminals to prey on unsuspecting victims, and this report shows how extensive these types of crime have become," James E. Finch, former Assistant Director of the FBI's Cyber Division, said of a recent IC3 collection of cyber crime information.

The range of crimes committed in cyberspace is mind-boggling. It includes auction fraud, work-at-home cons, credit card fraud, theft of **intellectual property**, hacking, identity theft, and other run-of-the-mill scams like get-rich-quick schemes and fake contests. Some of these crimes are committed in local areas, while others are nationwide or worldwide operations. The Internet has eliminated geographic boundaries and makes travel to commit a crime unnecessary.

As Assistant Director of the FBI's Cyber Division, Shawn Henry is in charge of overseeing the FBI's fight against cyber crime, including its programs that investigate espionage (spying) and terrorism.

Shameless Criminals

Just how **brazen** are these cyber con artists? The FBI received a report recently that a growing number of fraudulent emails have been circulating around the Internet making it appear as if the FBI itself is endorsing certain activities, such as lotteries, or that the agency is behind urgent notifications of inheritances that require people to release their private financial information. These emails use the FBI seal, banners, and letterhead. Some even contain the picture of FBI Director Robert S. Mueller III. The emails claim to be from both domestic and international FBI offices. The truth behind these emails is that the FBI never endorses or vouches for the validity of any type of contests or lotteries and never notifies people about inheritances. The emails are phony.

The FBI points to the phony emails as a prime example of the lengths to which cyber criminals will go to **ply** their trade, and the Bureau cautions the public to be wary of any unsolicited emails they receive that claim to have the endorsement of the FBI. The scam also shows that no one and no organizations are immune from being victimized by cyber crooks. In the case of these phony emails, the FBI itself is actually being victimized because the law enforcement agency's name and reputation are being fraudulently used and misrepresented by

FAST FACTS

More than 1 billion people around the world are online every day, giving **cyber criminals** a wide array of victims across the globe.

cyber con artists. Any such emails should be reported to the IC3 (*http://www.ic3.gov/default.aspx*).

The IC3 has received roughly 200,000 complaints a year over the past four years, with financial losses steadily rising every year and now topping the $240 million mark annually. Since the IC3 began keeping statistics about cyber crime in the year 2000, more than 1 million complaints have been recorded, leading to hundreds of thousands of criminal investigations and prosecutions.

An Underreported Crime

Former Assistant Director Finch said this about the report indicating the number of reports of cyber crime per year:

> What this report does not show is how often this type of activity goes unreported. Filing a complaint through the IC3 is the best way to alert law enforcement authorities of Internet crime.

While FBI investigations reveal that a large percentage of cyber criminals reside in the United States, a significant number of perpetrators live in Britain, Canada, Nigeria, Romania, and Italy. Up until recently, cyber criminals in foreign countries were thought of as untouchable because they were seemingly beyond the reach of U.S. law enforcement officials. The major reason for this was that some of the countries where these criminals set up operations often did not have laws pertaining to cyber crime. In foreign countries that did have laws to combat computer crime, the laws were usually weak or the police in those countries didn't have the know-how, the resources, or the desire to enforce those laws.

In the last few decades, the Internet has connected Western Europe and North America with regions of the world that previously seemed politically and geographically isolated, such as Eastern Europe and parts of Africa and the Middle East. These connections have increased the incidence of cyber crime on a global scale. They have also provided, however, greater cooperation among law enforcers worldwide.

Recently, however, the Department of Justice has begun training and equipping police in countries such as Romania and Nigeria, and the agency has forged stronger ties between nations in tracking down leads on notorious cyber villains. FBI teams have been going abroad and, with the help of police in these foreign countries, have been conducting successful investigations of cyber crimes of all kinds and proving that these crooks can be tracked down, apprehended, and convicted.

The National Strategy to Secure Cyberspace emphasizes the importance of a global approach to battling cyber crime, noting that problems in cyberspace in one continent can easily spread to another. The United States' strategy for protecting cyberspace calls for the sharing of information between nations to aid in the capture and prosecution of cyber crooks. The strategy also notes that, without this global cooperation, efforts to keep cyberspace safe will fall short.

CHAPTER 2 Cyber Criminals and Their Victims

Just as there is no single way to describe all burglars, bank robbers, car thieves, and muggers, no single profile fits all cyber criminals—or the people they choose to victimize, for that matter. But computers and cyberspace have allowed criminals to target many victims at one time, and even if only a few folks fall prey to the criminal's lure, the crime spree is underway, and the scheme is working.

The profile of the cyber criminal has changed greatly over the course of the past decade or so. Before the start of the 21st century, cyber crime was more of a nuisance than anything else. A teenager might hack into the computer system of a local business just to show his friends that he could

This young man is shown at an event in which participants compete to successfully hack into people's computers. Hacking was once considered by many to be a relatively small problem affecting only a few systems or networks. Today it has grown into a major type of cyber crime. It threatens the privacy, finances, and security of people, companies, and entire countries.

do it. After some detective work, the hacker would be tracked down, and police would make an arrest. Usually, local police were the only ones involved in the case. The penalties for the youthful offender were not usually very severe—perhaps a fine, **restitution**, or community service. Once the break-in was discovered, computer security experts would be called to install some simple computer security programs to make sure the business' computer would not be violated again.

Certainly, the business owner suffered some financial loss and computer downtime as information technology (IT) professionals worked to correct the problem, but these types of hackers were not thought of as vicious criminals or **diabolical** terrorists. Times have changed dramatically, however, and with that, the perception of computer crime.

Now most businesses have email, Web sites, and a presence in cyberspace, making them vulnerable to cyber criminals. The same is true of individuals. A person who might lock her car all the time to prevent it from being stolen, or have heavy-duty locks installed on her home's doors to prevent a break-in, might have a completely unprotected computer system or be totally unaware of the latest computer scams or viruses circulating in cyberspace. In addition, because computer criminals are so sophisticated, someone can be victimized and not even know it.

Who Are Cyber Criminals?

There is some uncertainty over the gender of specific cyber criminals, because victims rarely come face-to-face or even hear the voice of the person who is victimizing them. Most contact is made through email or through the Web. Sometimes the gender of the criminal is not known until an arrest is made, according to the FBI. Still, judging from what IC3 statistics are available, the vast majority of cyber criminals are believed to be male (75.2 percent).

Cyber criminals are usually in their mid-20s to mid-30s and are very savvy about computers. Many of these criminals have used computers all their lives and are keenly aware of how easy it is to conceal one's identity in cyberspace.

The geographical location of the perpetrator is usually unknown, unless it is mentioned in an email to the victim. Those references almost always prove to be false, but when perpetrators operating in the United States are tracked down, the IC3 statistics show that over 50 percent of them reside in California, Florida, Georgia, Illinois, New York, Pennsylvania, or Texas—all large states with densely populated areas.

Victims often don't realize how little they really know about the person committing the crime against them until they catch on to the scam. Most of the time, the victim is giving out truthful information about himself or herself to an unknown person. That criminal, in turn, is giving out false information. The perpetrator lies about everything—from his name and where he is located, to the deal he is offering and the company he may claim to represent.

Whom Do They Target?

Nearly 70 percent of cyber crime victims are between the ages of 20 and 49. Statistics show that the breakdown is nearly equal between the age groups of 20 to 29, 30 to 39, and 40 to 49, although those 40 to 49 are victimized slightly more than the others. Most people in these age groups have computers at work and at home and are comfortable using them. However, these victims are far less knowledgeable about computers than the perpetrators who target them and are a bit more trusting of the technology than they should be.

Cyber criminals also pick on people who may be lonely (taken in by romance fraud); those on fixed or limited incomes who need to save money on products and services (lured in by fraudulent get-rich-quick schemes); and people looking for jobs (deceived by bogus job-hunting leads). They also take advantage of people's good nature by running scams to collect money for phony, nonexistent causes and charities.

What Are They After?

Most of the time, cyber criminals are **trolling** for personal information that they can use to commit more crimes—such as identity theft—but sometimes they simply try to get money from their victims. What these crooks are after are credit card account numbers, bank account numbers, Social Security numbers, birth dates, and other personal information that can be used to steal identities and make illegal purchases.

David Kernell (center) is shown leaving court in October 2008 after pleading not guilty to charges of hacking into the email account of Republican vice presidential nominee Sarah Palin. At the time of the attack on Palin's email, the hacker claimed that his intention was to hurt her campaign.

Individuals are not the only victims of cyber crime. Many businesses, nonprofit organizations, colleges, financial institutions, hospitals and other health care providers, and even government agencies fall prey to these computer thieves as well.

When cyber crooks break into commercial computer systems, they are usually looking for trade secrets and carefully guarded ideas in development to sell to a company's competitors, either in the United States or overseas. As a result of cyberspace, all types of information are now vulnerable to theft and are worth money in various ways to tech-savvy crooks.

Why Is Cyber Crime So Tempting to Crooks?

Why does computer crime have so much appeal to the criminal mind? According to Scott O'Neal, chief of the FBI's Computer Intrusion Section:

> Criminals saw the early hackers and said, wow, that's a lot less dangerous than drug trafficking. The problem is so vast and so **systemic** that people need to be prepared for the worst. Companies need to assume that they'll be a victim.

Going after a business by breaking into its computer infrastructure and stealing personal information about clients and employees is a much faster way for criminals to get what they are seeking than conning individuals one by one. Sometimes cyber lawbreakers use this information themselves, and sometimes they sell it to other crooks who use the information to embark on more criminal activity.

Organized Crime in Cyberspace

The FBI reports seeing a troubling new trend recently. There is much more organized crime in cyberspace than ever before.

Online organized crime is not the traditional organized crime with which everyone has become familiar over the years. This is a new type of organized crime—gangs of people from far-flung corners of the world who get together online to pull off major cyber crimes.

Organized by several people who have criminal backgrounds and an idea of what type of crime they want to commit, these gangs set out to find people with computer know-how, people who have a way to sell identities on the street, and still more criminals who know how to sell credit card and bank information. Once all of these pieces are put in place, a massive worldwide crime ring—one that can be exceedingly hard to pin down—is set in motion.

Danielle Helms is the mother of Kristin Danielle Helms, a 15-year-old who killed herself after she was sexually molested by a predator she met online. In this photo, Helms prepares to speak at an FBI news conference called to announce a round-up of suspected **pedophiles** in Los Angeles in 2007. Her message to parents is that they should monitor their children's computer use closely to be sure kids aren't sharing too much information on the Internet.

Since the ring is organized in cyberspace, many of the ring's members do not even know who the other members are. They have probably never met face-to-face. So if some ring members are caught, they legitimately cannot give the FBI the names and locations of all their partners in cyber crime.

Reluctance to Report

One of the biggest problems in fighting cyber crime is that victims—both individuals and businesses—often don't report the crime. Individuals may be embarrassed that they fell for a scam, and they therefore tend to suffer in silence. Often they refuse to tell even close family members that they were victims of a computer crime. Beyond this, these victims may realize that they have very little information about the cyber crook who victimized them. This makes them feel it isn't worth contacting law enforcement about the incident.

WANTED
BY THE FBI

CYBER CRIMES

✉ Get e-mail updates when cyber crimes fugitives information is updated.
Get news feeds about current fugitives

Saad Echouafni
Computer Intrusion

Tobechi Enyinna Onwuhara
Conspiracy to Commit Bank Fraud

Jie Dong
Wire Fraud

Edwin Andres Pena
Computer Intrusion; Wire Fraud

Although it is not very likely that any of these suspects will be seen actually committing a cyber crime, the FBI counts on the public to provide tips that might lead to an arrest. In this sense, cyber criminals are treated the same as any others, with their faces and biographies prominently posted on the FBI's Web site.

To the FBI, however, nothing could be farther from the truth. Every complaint that the agency gets helps operatives come closer to solving a crime. The more complaints that FBI special agents receive about similar crimes, the better able they are to establish a pattern of crime. Victims may not see a clue in the information they are giving law enforcement, but a trained special agent might just spot something important. A key piece of evidence can come from something that a victim might think is meaningless. In a situation where many of the criminals are relying on anonymity, every complaint can add a piece to the puzzle. So the FBI urges all victims to report cyber crime to the IC3 or directly to the FBI itself.

Businesses, like individuals, are also hesitant to report incidents of cyber crime. But embarrassment over having been conned is just a small part of their reluctance. The main reason companies generally keep quiet about cyber crime committed against them comes from their fear of negative publicity. A company identified as the victim of a security **breach** could be viewed as **negligent**. People may think the company did not do enough to prevent the break-in. One recent study showed that only 29 percent of companies,

FAST FACTS

The Web site called Looks Too Good to Be True (www.lookstoogoodtobetrue.com) keeps people up to date on how to avoid becoming victims of computer fraud and scams.

universities, and government agencies have reported computer **intrusions**.

FBI Director Robert S. Mueller III continues to stress the importance of businesses reporting any breaches of security. Businesses should report if only to give the FBI valuable information about an ongoing pattern of cyber criminal activity. Says Mueller:

> We know that [businesses] have practical concerns about reporting breaches of security, but we must find a way to stop these attacks. Maintaining a code of silence will not benefit you or your company in the long run.

The FBI encourages companies, universities, and government agencies to work side by side to stop crime in cyberspace. "Working side-by-side is not just the best option; it is the only option," Mueller says.

Online Bullying

Another disturbing pattern in cyber criminal activity is the growing number of crimes being committed against children.

While the effects of online bullying may not be as apparent as those of bullying in school or on the playground, they can be just as harmful.

This illustration is from the FBI's "Parent's Guide to Internet Safety." The guide is available for viewing and downloading online at http://www.fbi.gov/publi cations/pguide/pguidee.htm.

FAST FACTS

One way the FBI is responding to cyber crimes against children is to teach parents how to protect youngsters from cyber villains. The bureau has published "A Parent's Guide to Internet Safety." It is available free of charge online.

Often these crimes are committed by peers. In 2008 the Rochester Institute of Technology (RIT) conducted a survey of 40,000 adolescents about computer bullying. The survey showed that 59 percent of 11- to 14-year-olds who were bullied online called those who were bullying them "friends" or youths they knew well. The victims were receiving hateful and even threatening messages repeatedly through email.

Sam McQuade heads the graduate program at RIT's Center for Multidisciplinary Studies. He said the study shows that "children are most frequently preying on each other online—and their parents rarely have any idea it's happening." The study also showed that nearly 75 percent of 12- to 14-year-olds surf the Internet with little or no supervision.

WORKING TOGETHER WORKS

With more than 26,100 members, InfraGard (see logo below) is an example of a cooperative information and analysis network. It is dedicated to combating and preventing cyber crime. InfraGard is also an FBI program. It has local groups, called chapters, throughout the country, which are linked to the FBI's 56 field offices.

The program began in 1996 in the FBI's Cleveland field office. It grew into a national effort by 1998. Its members include businesses, schools and universities, law enforcement groups, government agencies, and interested people. The group's goal is to make cyberspace safer for everyone. InfraGard alerts members to the latest computer intrusions, letting them know how to protect themselves.

Each chapter has an FBI special agent coordinator and meets on a regular basis. Chapter members discuss issues and threats of particular concern to them. They also learn about the concerns of other members and see what they are doing about them. The FBI is hoping that programs like InfraGard will have two main effects. First, it should prevent computer intrusions by providing members with the latest information on how to avoid them. Second, InfraGard should encourage those who are attacked to report the incident so others will not fall victim to the same thing.

Information is shared by local chapters. But it also is passed on and shared at the national level. Information sharing is done on a timely basis, which is a key to InfraGard's success.

One of InfraGard's biggest accomplishments is that most of its local chapters have developed an emergency plan to implement alternative systems in the event of a massive attack on the information infrastructure. Those plans are constantly being updated to keep pace with changing technology.

The FBI has always advised parents not to let their children go online unsupervised. The alarming bullying statistics compiled by the FBI is one matter. But the bureau also has long been on the trail of people seeking to exploit children through online contact. The FBI has always considered the Innocent Images National Initiative (IINI) one of its most important programs. A part of the FBI's Cyber Division, Innocent Images is a coordinated effort to combat the exploitation of children online. Unfortunately, FBI special agents find no shortage of predators lurking in cyberspace.

FAST FACTS

In 1996, when the FBI first launched its Innocent Images National Initiative (see logo below) to catch online child predators, it investigated a total of 113 cases. Today thousands of new cases are opened every year. In the 10-year period from 1996 to 2005, the program obtained 4,822 convictions of online child predators.

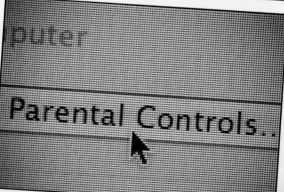

The FBI urges parents to keep as close a watch on their children's online activities as they would on where kids go outdoors.

CHAPTER 3
FBI Special Agents in Cyberspace

Having solid leads, good tips, and reliable, up-to-date information are important in fighting street crime. But they are just as important in battling and solving cyber crime. That is why the FBI urges people to come forward with any information they might have that could help solve crime, especially cyber crime. (Start off by connecting with the Bureau's home page at *www.fbi.gov* and then look for links to contacting the FBI or providing tips). Someone might overhear something, see something, or have a key piece of evidence that might help law enforcement officials crack a crime spree in cyberspace.

This map shows the nations participating in the Strategic Alliance Cyber Crime Working Group. This group plans to have cyber cops from all over the world sharing information and forensic tools, raising public awareness, holding joint training sessions, and setting up a joint international task force made up of cyber law enforcement investigators from the countries in the alliance.

The Strategic Alliance Cyber Crime Working Group
Lead Law Enforcement Agencies

Royal Canadian Mounted Police

UNITED KINGDOM

CANADA

Serious Organise Crime Agency

UNITED STATES

FBI*

Australian Federal Police

New Zealand Police

AUSTRALIA

NEW ZEALAND

*Current chair of the g

With this in mind, the FBI believes it is more important than ever to build a good relationship with the law-abiding online community. In this updated version of the cop on the beat—the police officer who patrols a particular neighborhood and knows and is trusted by everyone in that community—the "neighborhood" is the virtual community of cyberspace.

The FBI has partnered with a number of organizations to build that relationship. Their efforts have two goals. The first is to get cyber crime prevention information out to the public. The second is to help protect individuals, businesses, schools, government agencies, hospitals, and other nonprofit institutions from cyber criminals.

International Initiative

In September 2006, the FBI hosted a meeting in Washington, D.C., of law enforcement officials specializing in cyber crime. Cyber cops from Canada, New Zealand, Australia, and the United Kingdom met with U.S. cyber cops. At the meeting, they formed the Strategic Alliance Cyber Crime Working Group. This partnership is dedicated to fighting cyber crime on a global level.

The FBI also works closely with the National Cyber-Forensics and Training Alliance (NCFTA) in Pittsburgh. FBI special agents are assigned to NCFTA and work side by side with agents from Homeland Security and U.S. postal inspectors. NCFTA gets information and assistance from more than 600 partner groups, such as private businesses and antifraud organizations. The group also works with students and researchers from the highly regarded Computer Emergency

Response Team Coordination Center at Carnegie Mellon University, also in Pittsburgh.

The partnership work is already paying off. Based on NCFTA's hard work, law enforcement officials have been able to track down many online scams. Online groups claiming to raise money for people displaced by Hurricane Katrina in 2005 are one example. Drawing information from many sources, cyber cops put an end to these and other scams.

Partnerships Enhance Security

These partnerships and joint efforts aid efforts to crack down on cyber crime and beef up national security. In the words of FBI Director Mueller:

> All of this makes us safer, certainly, than we were on September 11 [2001, when the World Trade Center and the Pentagon were attacked]. While I will say we are safer, that does not mean we are safe.

Police patrol a neighborhood ravaged by wildfires in Los Angeles. In 2007 and 2008, the National Cyber Forensics and Training Alliance (NCFTA) went after scammers supposedly raising money for victims of wildfires in southern California.

Cyber criminals find ways to exploit almost every innovation put in place to enhance the Internet for law-abiding citizens.

Take peer-to-peer networks (also known as *P2P*), for instance. These allow Internet users to link to computers around the world for effortless information sharing. By installing the proper free software, P2P-network users can share certain files in their computers with other P2P users and can get into the hard drive of another network member to download specific files.

Properly designed P2P software protects the private information on each member's hard drive. But in some cases, the software may be flawed. This could lead to unwanted breaches of a user's computer. The FBI urges people using this technology to learn all they can about the software they are installing. That way, they can make sure that it is **configured** properly.

Peer-to-peer networks actually open computer files to millions of people. That means hackers can take advantage of the technology and infect a person's computer with worms and viruses. But that is not all.

Cyber crooks use peer-to-peer systems to steal copyrighted material, trade secrets, and ideas under development. In one recent case, a Virginia man set up a peer-to-peer network for the purpose of making available and selling hundreds of materials that were copyright protected against piracy of any sort. His P2P attracted more than 125,000 users and led to the illegal downloading of more than one million copies of about 700 movies plus illegal copies of expensive copyrighted software, video games, and music—all before they were available in retail stores or movie theaters. Any distribution of these materials without permission violates federal law.

The use of peer-to-peer technology to distribute pornography is also a major federal crime. Perpetrators often send children pornography labeled as music or a computer game. The files may contain graphic images or messages calculated to get children to exchange emails. Worse, the files may encourage the child to meet with the sender. In this case, the sender claims to be looking for a friend, but he is actually a child predator. In several recent cases, investigators busted distributors and receivers of child pornography in New York, Arizona, California, Wyoming, Nebraska, and Texas. In the Texas case, the pornographer was also charged with sexually assaulting a six-year-old child in Colorado.

The FBI warns parents to be vigilant about monitoring what files children are opening on the Internet.

So FBI special agents continue to hone their skills in the never-ending battle to secure cyberspace. The most highly trained cyber detectives the FBI has are assigned to Cyber Action Teams. These are better known as CATs. CATs are small teams of special agents, analysts, code breakers, and computer forensics experts.

The CATs are a little like the minutemen who helped the American colonies fight the British during the American Revolution. They stand ready to travel, on a moment's notice, anywhere in the country or around the world to pursue a cyber threat. CATs bring with them enough computer investigative equipment, including forensic supplies, for a six-month-long investigation. Additional supplies are only a phone call away.

These teams constantly gather vital information about the latest cyber crime trends and computer intrusions, even when they are not on the road or working on a specific case. These teams keep up-to-the-minute data on terrorist-related activity in cyberspace and work around the clock to **foil** threats to the nation's security or its information infrastructure.

A Quick Response

In 2005, the Zotob worm invaded and disabled computer systems everywhere. The FBI tracked the culprits to Turkey and Morocco and, with the permission of those countries' governments, dispatched two CATs to the site. Working with their **counterparts** in Turkey and Morocco, the FBI special agents were able to **ferret out** the perpetrators. About a week after arriving in the two countries, arrests were made. With each case, members of these specially trained teams gain more

This map displays the six regions into which the Bureau's international operations teams are grouped. In the case of the FBI's tracking of the Zotob "worm," Cyber Action Teams (CATs) worked with international agencies through FBI offices in Turkey (part of Eurasia on this map) and Morocco (in North Africa).

knowledge and insight into the mind of the cyber criminal.

The FBI believes the best way to tackle cyber crime and threats is to approach perpetrators from all different angles. That means having a large number of investigators to identify threats and monitor the activity connected with each of those threats. Eventually, the FBI is hoping that these trained investigators will be able to predict where threats are likely to come from. This requires that agents develop intelligence networks and constantly come up with new ways to assess the information they receive in order to stop intrusions before they happen. That has been the goal of the National Cyber Investigative Joint Task Force (NCIJTF), launched in 2007.

The NCIJTF is a **collaborative** venture. Through it, FBI agents work with U.S. intelligence professionals and members of other federal agencies, including the Department of Homeland Security and the Secret Service. The Secret Service was given this assignment because of that agency's work in

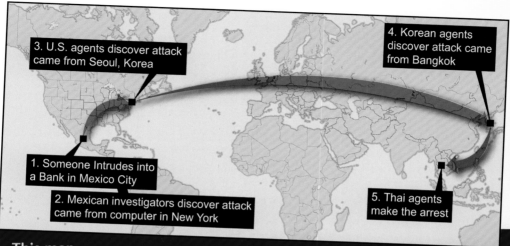

3. U.S. agents discover attack came from Seoul, Korea

4. Korean agents discover attack came from Bangkok

1. Someone Intrudes into a Bank in Mexico City

2. Mexican investigators discover attack came from computer in New York

5. Thai agents make the arrest

This map
illustrates how a cyber attack in one part of the world might be solved through a network of agencies cooperating to make an arrest in another part of the world. In this scenario, a cyber crook hacks into a bank in Mexico. Mexican authorities trace the computer used in the attack to New York City. FBI agents discover that the New York computer is linked to one in South Korea. They notify Korean authorities, who learn that the attack originated in Thailand, where they make the arrest.

battling counterfeiting, which also includes any attack on the nation's financial system from cyberspace. The FBI has always said that a violent attack was not the only threat to our nation's security. Attacks on the country's financial or information infrastructure could be just as destructive, the Bureau believes. Cyberspace makes such attacks possible. Because of that, investigating threats of this kind is an FBI priority.

Cyber Crime Task Force

Another example of FBI special agents forging a valuable partnership is the Cyber Crime Task Force. Versions of this task force exist in many FBI field offices. One of the most significant and advanced task forces was established in May

2008 by the FBI's Indianapolis field office. It brings together state and local law enforcement officials in Indiana. It also taps into Purdue University's Cyber Forensics Lab, plus Purdue's Center for Education and Research in Information Assurance and Security (CERIAS). Purdue University, in West Lafayette, Indiana, has worked with the FBI for years. But this cooperative effort will officially allow the FBI to call on Purdue's computer experts. They will be allowed to help with cases around the world. Through CERIAS, Purdue has become a leader in information security. The FBI is also impressed with the work that has been done at Purdue in the area of **digital forensics**.

Said CERIAS Director Eugene H. Spafford at the time of the announced partnership between Purdue and the FBI:

> Cyber crime is a growing threat to society. There are so many facets to cyber crime, and it costs the U.S. economy to the tune of tens of billions of dollars. We're glad to provide our resources to the FBI.

Regional Computer Forensic Labs

To help fight cyber crime, the FBI has set up 14 computer forensic labs. The first lab opened in San Diego in 2000. Work there helped solve so many cyber crime–related cases that the FBI began opening labs across the country. These labs always partner with state and local law enforcement agencies and any area schools that might be able to help in the global effort to secure cyberspace.

The Regional Computer Forensic Laboratory (RCFL) program sets up these state-of-the-art labs. The labs are equipped with the latest computer forensic equipment. They also have highly trained personnel, who in turn train thousands of other law enforcement officers throughout the region. The experts teach the officers how to gather evidence and investigate a cyber-related crime.

FBI Director Mueller called the RCFL program a vital part of the fight against cyber crime. The work done in the labs supports law enforcement at all levels. Said Mueller:

> By combining the extraordinary talents and resources of law enforcement agencies at all levels, our ability to investigate criminals and detect and prevent acts of terrorism becomes considerably more **robust**.

In addition to the RCFL program's crime-solving capabilities, people at the labs also conduct research and develop technologies to combat the ever-expanding network of cyber criminals. Once a discovery is made, the new technology is repeatedly tested. If it is a proven success, it is recommended to the FBI's other labs for use in specific cases.

For instance, with technology developed in the San Diego lab detectives can go into a computer hard drive and secure the contents so it will not be damaged or altered in any way. This allows investigators to read and reread all the files on the hard drive without running the risk that evidence will be lost as it is sifted through. This concern often hindered investigations in the past.

How It Works

Here is how an RCFL lab can make a big difference in a criminal case. A Dallas man was shot to death in his own

With the right data-recovery technology and expertise, even a home computer as badly burned as this one may be coaxed into giving up valuable information from its damaged hard drive.

home. The murderer, apparently afraid of something in the man's computer, set the computer on fire before leaving the home. The Dallas police brought the badly burned and mostly melted remains of the computer to the FBI lab in North Texas. **Undaunted** by the condition of the nearly **obliterated** computer, experts at the lab figured out a way to get into the computer by replacing its melted circuit board with one of the exact same model. They also found a floppy disk that was twisted, melted, and stuck inside the computer.

Computer forensic experts carefully removed the disk from the computer. They then took the disk out of its destroyed casing and put it into another casing. The experts then cleaned the disk over and over again. After each cleaning, they tried to retrieve the information on it. Finally, their persistence paid off: After countless cleanings, the disk yielded the vital digital evidence necessary to solve the case.

This case is just one example of how police investigations are conducted in cyberspace. It all comes down to good old-fashioned, relentless, determined police work—with a bit of a modern twist.

CHAPTER 4

Schemes, Scams, and Flimflams

Creativity abounds in cyberspace when it comes to con artists seeking to scam innocent victims out of their hard-earned money or personal information over the Internet. New scams are being devised all the time. Old scams are being reworked and updated. And new victims are joining the cyber community every day.

This email falsely claims to be from the Internal Revenue Service (IRS). By offering the recipient a fake "refund" under the Economic Stimulus Act of 2008, the sender hopes to gain important information that may lead to identity theft and scamming the recipient out of money. One certain sign of such a letter being false is its being sent by email— something the IRS would never do.

Over 130 million Americans will receive refunds as part of President Bush program to jumpstart the economy. Our records indicate that you are qualified to receive the 2008 Economic Stimulus Refund.

The fastest and easiest way to receive your refund is by direct deposit to your checking/savings account. Please follow the link and fill out the form and submit before May 10, 2008, to ensure that your refund will be processed as soon as possible.

Submitting your form on May 10, 2008, or later means that your refund will be delayed due to the volume of requests we anticipate for the Economic Stimulus Refund.

To access Economic Stimulus Refund, please click here.

So just how fast do these cyber crooks come up with ideas for new schemes? A good example is the scam that came out right after President George W. Bush signed into law the Economic Stimulus Act of 2008. This act provided for tax rebate checks for millions of Americans. Shortly after this, emails were sent to thousands of Americans, supposedly from the Internal Revenue Service (IRS). The email claimed that the quickest way to get the tax rebate was through direct deposit. These bogus emails then directed taxpayers to a link to sign up for their refund.

The truth is that the IRS never sent out any such emails. The link embedded in the message was to a fraudulent site designed to gather personal information from people who fell for the scam. The cyber crooks used a warning to increase their odds of getting people to go along with the con. The warning, meant to frighten readers, said that a delay in supplying the requested information would mean a longer wait for the rebate check. Information gathered at the fraudulent site was then used to get credit cards in the victim's name and make unauthorized purchases. Identity theft was also committed with the information collected in this scam. Within a few weeks after the scam was started, the cyber crooks had the information they wanted and were on to a new con.

Schemes, scams, and flimflams in cyberspace are growing faster than the technology itself. Here is a rundown on some more cyber cons.

Jury Summons

The fraudulent jury summons scheme gets people to open an email because they think they are being called for jury duty. The notice instructs the recipient to click through to get important information about where and when he or she is supposed to serve.

When the victim follows the links, a malicious code is released. The victim's computer is infected. Sometimes these notices ask the victim to respond with personal information, including financial data.

The emails look official. They include case numbers, code numbers, the address of the court, and even the court seal or the actual name of an issuing court officer.

The Nigerian Letter

One of the most popular scams is the "Nigerian letter." In this scam, the victim gets an email from someone who claims to be a government official in Nigeria. The author of the email asks for help in getting some money—which he either saved or inherited—out of the country. Recently, these emails have been coming from foreign countries besides Nigeria, but the plea for help is similar.

The victim is offered a large amount of money in exchange for help with the transaction. Sometimes the victim is asked to put up some money or provide personal information to

DEAR SIR

REQUEST FOR URGENT CONFIDENTIAL BUSINESS RELATIONSHIP_RE:TRANSFER OF US$21.32M US DOLLARS INTO YOUR ACCOUNT.

WE WANT A RELIABLE PERSON WHO COULD ASSIST US TO TRANSFER THE SUM OF THIRTY-ONE MILLION, FIVE HUNDRED THOUSAND U.S. DOLLARS ONLY (US$31.5M) INTO HIS ACCOUNT.

I HAVE BEEN DELEGATED AS A MATTER OF TRUST BY MY COLLEAGUES TO LOOK FOR AN OVERSEAS PARTNER INTO WHOSE ACCOUNT WE WOULD TRANSFER THE SUM OF US$21,320,000.00(TWENTY ONE MILLION, THREE HUNDRED AND TWENTY THOUSAND U.S DOLLARS). THIS RESULTS FROM AN OVER-INVOICE BILL IN VARIOUS MINISTRIES. WE HAVE IDENTIFIED A LOT OF INFLATED CONTRACT FUNDS WHICH ARE PRESENTLY FLOATING IN THE CENTRAL BANK OF NIGERIA READY FOR PAYMENT.

HOWEVER, BY VIRTUE OF OUR POSITION AS CIVIL SERVANTS, WE CANNOT ACQUIRE THIS MONEY IN OUR NAMES. HENCE WE ARE WRITING YOU THIS LETTER. WE HAVE AGREED TO SHARE THE MONEY THUS; 1. 20% FOR THE ACCOUNT OWNER 2. 70% FOR US (THE OFFICIALS) 3. 10% TO BE USED IN SETTLING TAXATION AND ALL LOCAL AND FOREIGN EXPENSES. IT IS FROM THE 70% THAT WE WISH TO COMMENCE THE IMPORTATION BUSINESS.

LET HONESTY AND TRUST BE OUR WATCHWORD THROUGHOUT THIS TRANSACTION AND YOUR PROMPT REPLY WILL BE HIGHLY APPRECIATED.

BEST REGARDS, DR. OBI PATRICK.

An example of a typical "Nigerian letter" asking for help in a fraudulent "business relationship."

prove he or she can be trusted. Other times the victim is asked to send money to help pay taxes or other expenses before the inheritance or savings can be distributed. Often the victim is asked for bank account information so his or her share of the money can be deposited directly into the bank.

Naturally, no money is ever forthcoming. Instead, the victim's personal information is used to steal his or her identity. Most people realize that this is a scam as soon as they get the email. But millions of dollars are lost each year by victims who believe the email is a legitimate opportunity to share in a **windfall**.

Natural Disaster Charity Scams

Almost every time a natural disaster strikes the United States or even a foreign country, cyber con artists come up with a new scam. They approach good-hearted people, asking them to give money to help the disaster victims. Millions of dollars are donated to these phony charities. But none of the money ever goes to help the victims of the natural disasters.

> This is to inform you of the release of money winnings to you. Your email was randomly selected as the winner and therefore you have been approved for a lump sum payout of $500,000.00.
>
> To begin your lottery claim, please contact the processing company selected to process your winnings.

It seems like exciting news. Your name or email has been selected out of thousands or even millions of others to win a huge amount of money in a lottery drawing. But if it's a drawing for which you never registered, beware. It may be a scam to get personal information that can be used to steal your identity.

Cyber criminals put together and store large lists of email addresses. Often they have stolen these addresses through other cyber crimes. As soon as a disaster occurs, they send out heart-wrenching emails pleading for donations. Keep in mind that emails are rarely used to gather donations in response to these types of disasters. Relief efforts usually are run by well-known national or international relief organizations such as the Red Cross. These organizations ask people to contact them and make donations directly. They make their pleas through the mass media, such as daily newspapers and television stations.

Sometimes local groups do organize drives for victims of natural disasters. Groups such as houses of worship, community service organizations, and others do like to help. But, again, such organizations reach out to donors through public means. These may include stories or ads in the local media, announcements during weekly meetings or prayer services, or signs posted outside their buildings to inform people of their efforts.

The FBI reports that fraudulent cyber schemes to raise money are launched whenever tragedies occur. Even events such as the deadly collapse of a bridge in Minneapolis and the Virginia Tech shootings, both of which happened in 2007, had

FAST FACTS

How to spot a phony: Most emails sent by scam artists (such as those in this book) contain spelling, punctuation, and grammatical errors.

Students attend a one-year anniversary memorial for victims of the shootings at Virginia Tech. Scammers eager to cash in on the tragedy worked the Internet, trying to convince well-intentioned people to donate money to phony charities.

thieves online, eager to capitalize on the misfortune of others. On April 17, 2007, one day after the Virginia Tech tragedy in which a gunman killed 32 people before taking his own life, one **entrepreneur**, in an effort to create interest in his own Web site, posted a message stating that a similar attack would occur at San Diego State University. Although the threat turned out to be a hoax, the person who operated the Web site was arrested, convicted, and sentenced to six months in jail for "sending a threatening communication over the Internet."

Phishing

Phishing is a scam for gathering personal information for illegal uses. Incidents of it are rising at an alarming rate. These scams have become commonplace because cyber thieves can target so many people at once. Currently, there are so many phishing scenarios in use that the FBI finds it almost impossible to alert the public about all of them.

In a typical phishing scam, a person is notified by email that she has to reactivate one of her accounts. It may be a credit card, a debit card, a checking account, a savings account, or some type of bank account. Sometimes the victim is told that these accounts have expired

The more people use credit cards and debit cards, the more vulnerable they become to phishing. In this type of scam, victims are convinced to give vital personal information over the Internet, supposedly for the purpose of renewing their accounts.

and need to be updated. The emails tell the target to call a phone number to respond to the email. When the victim calls the number, someone using the bank's name answers the phone. Sometimes machines handle the calls, and the victim is asked to leave the information on the automated system. On other occasions, a person answers the phone and takes down the information. It all depends on how sophisticated the criminal operation is.

Some of the emails are sent on phony bank letterhead. These notices may even inform people that, "for their own protection," they must call only the number in the email. With a touch of **irony** and to make the scam email look even more real, the notice actually warns the unsuspecting victims about fraud. It states that "for their own security" they should never give out any personal information over the Internet.

Rogue Bots

A bot is an automated program. (Its name is a shortened version of robot.) It can do repetitive computer work at a much faster pace than a person and never complains about doing that type of work. Meanwhile, a person can be doing something much more important. That is why bots were invented, and they were a welcome addition to the world of technology.

Bots are often used for malicious purposes, however. When someone puts bots on the prowl in a certain way, they can pose a threat to the nation's information infrastructure. The scheme usually works like this: A criminal bot "herder" puts together a network of "compromised" computers—computers in which bots have been placed by the herder. The **bot herder** takes over the computers of unsuspecting people through the use of viruses or worms that are secretly released by emails. Once a computer is infected, it can then be remotely controlled and used for criminal activities such as identity theft or fraud. Some botnets (networks of bots) control tens of thousands of computers.

In one case the FBI recently solved, a bot herder in Seattle used a huge botnet to deliver tens of millions of spam (unwanted or inappropriate) email messages to users whose computers he'd compromised in order to advertise his own Web site, which offered services and products. Others have used their botnets for far more serious purposes, infecting computers in hospitals and businesses in order to disable their operating systems or steal data.

What is really worrisome is that this activity can happen without computer users knowing it. "The majority of victims are not even aware that their computer has been compromised or their personal information exploited," said James Finch, former Assistant Director of the FBI's Cyber Division:

An attacker gains control by infecting the computer with a virus or other malicious code, and the computer continues to operate normally. Citizens can protect themselves from botnets and the associated schemes by practicing strong computer security habits to reduce the risk that your computer will be compromised.

FAST FACTS

Within three years of the terrorist attacks of September 11, 2001, more than 150,000 people applied to become special agents with the FBI. Only 2,200 of those applicants measured up to the Bureau's tough hiring standards, however, and were actually put on the job.

The FBI uses Operation Bot Roast to fight this kind of crime. This program disrupts botnets and arrests bot herders and others involved in these crimes. The FBI also reminds computer users that installing security systems will help prevent future botnet attacks. Unfortunately, a new security system may not identify or remove rogue bots that have already infected the computer.

Operation Bot Roast is symbolized on the FBI's Web site by this image of a bot herder's computer being "zapped" by the Bureau's new initiative. So far, the program has identified over one million computer addresses that have been invaded by rogue bots.

When it comes to cyber crime, the FBI believes this well-used expression: If it sounds too good to be true, it probably is. Internet users need to keep that in mind as well. That—and taking some security steps to protect online information—is the best way to avoid becoming a cyber crime victim.

The FBI uses its Web site (*www.fbi.gov*) and its links under "What We Investigate" and "Be Crime Smart" to help keep people alert and aware. The site is filled with tips on how to recognize computer scams. It also offers information on the latest technology to protect computers from intrusions. In the words of FBI Director Robert S. Mueller III, cyberspace is a place of great opportunity but also great peril:

> The Internet has opened up thousands of new roads for each of us—new ideas and information, new sights and sounds, new people and places. But the invaders—those whose intent is not enlightenment but exploitation and extremism—are marching right down those same roads to attack us in multiple ways.

Today people use the Internet for everything from buying products to finding romance and landing jobs. Such uses have become common. Because of this, it is important that people understand the pitfalls of using a computer for these purposes.

It is one way to avoid becoming a victim of cyber fraud.

Romance Fraud

For instance, people who are considering online dating should become familiar with romance scams. Many Web sites, including the FBI's, contain information about these frauds. The most common form of romance fraud involves preying on a lonely victim. Often this is a woman with whom the scammer has developed a relationship through a series of friendly emails. As the relationship grows, the scam artist will send a photo to the victim, supposedly of himself. But the photo is probably a picture of someone else. Such photos may be taken off someone else's Web site (without their knowledge)

FAST FACTS

According to the latest statistics, more than 70 percent of four-year-olds in the United States have used a computer at least one time in their lives.

One type of romance fraud involves convincing people from other countries to pay money to come to the United States and marry a U.S. citizen as a way of gaining citizenship themselves. In one recent case (represented at right on the FBI's Web site), the Bureau investigated and arrested two brothers who convinced people in the People's Republic of China to pay $40,000 each to become "engaged" to Chinese Americans who were paid to pose as their "fiancés." No weddings took place, and the victims' families lost their money.

Chinese Immigration Fraud

or even out of a clothing catalog. Eventually, the exchanges become affectionate as the cyber crook sets up his victim.

The Internet Crime Complaint Center (IC3) reports that the con artist usually claims to live far from the victim—often in another country. The two agree to meet, and the criminal convinces the victim that he needs money to cover his travel expenses. At this point he asks the victim to send him some money. Usually, the con artist proceeds to pocket the money and then claims that something terrible happened to him—and the money—on the way to the airport: He was mugged, and the money was stolen. He had a car accident and had to use the money the victim sent for medical expenses.

No matter what the story, the end result is always the same. The con needs more money, and the victim, who trusts the person with whom she has been exchanging emails, sends it. The scam goes on as long as the victim continues to send money.

Hit-man Scam

Cyber crooks also play off of people's fears. One scam that the FBI says has been going on for years seems transparently fake, and yet it is nasty and uses fear as its hook. In this scam, a victim gets an email from a person who claims to be hired to kill him. In the email, the victim is told that if he agrees to send a certain amount of money to a particular person or bank account, the killing will be called off. The victim is given a deadline by which the money has to be sent. He is warned that if he goes to the police he will be killed—even if the money is received on time.

This is a very profitable scam. Many people pay the money and do not call the police. If the victims had contacted the

Subject: Merry Xmas to you and stay alive...........

Attention,

I Want you to read this message very carefully, and keep the secret with you till further notice, You have no need of knowing who i am, where am from,till i make out a space for us to see, i have being paid $150, 000.00 in advance to terminate you with some reasons listed to me by my employer,its one i believe you call a friend and a Home Builder you do business everyday with,i have followed you closely for one week and tree days now and have seen that you are innocent of the accusetion,Do not contact the police or try to send a copy of this to them, because if you do i will know, and might be pushed to do what i have being paid to do,beside this the first time i turned out to be a betrayer in my job.

Now listen,i will arrange for us to see face to face but before that i need the amount of $150,000.00,you have nothing to be afraid of,i will come to your office or home, so determine when you wish we meet,do not set any camera to cover us or set up any tape to record our conversation,my employer is in my control now,$80, 000.00 will be paid to the account i will provide for you,after our conversation,i will give you the tape that contains his request for me to terminate you, which will be enough evidence for you to take him to court (if you wish to), then the balance will be paid. You don't need my phone contact for now till am assured you are ready to comply good. NOTE:I have you whole details. Lucky You.

A typical "hit-man" email.

police, they would have been told that the email was just part of an elaborate con game. No one was out to kill them. A new variation on this theme is an email warning that a family member will be kidnapped within 48 hours if a ransom is not paid. The email tells the recipient where to send the money and threatens to carry out the kidnapping if the police are notified.

Beware of Unsolicited Emails

The FBI warns all Internet users to be suspicious of unsolicited emails asking for personal information. Federal agencies do not ask for such information over the Internet. Sometimes such an email appears to come from the recipient's own bank or employer. It is worth taking the time to call the bank or employer to see if the email actually came from there. Cyber con artists often create phony Web sites—complete with corporate logos—that look amazingly similar to real ones. Then they send out emails telling unsuspecting people to go to the Web site. There they are instructed to leave personal and financial information. The cyber crooks then steal that information.

Legitimate businesses will not mind getting a phone call to verify that such information is needed. When calling to make sure an email request for information is genuine, people should call a number they know is connected with that business. It is best if the number is one that they have called before. Better yet, people should talk with someone whose voice they recognize. At a bank, for instance, they should talk to a teller or a branch manager they know.

Online Job Scams

People looking for jobs online should be careful, too. One online scheme posts a job but does not provide many details about it—not the job location, responsibilities, hours, or wages. But the ad asks the applicant to fill out an online application seeking all types of personal information. Among the "required fields" in this online form are the applicant's birth date and Social Security number. Sometimes it even asks for bank information, saying that the employer would make payments directly to the bank account once the job started. This information is then used to commit other crimes, including using the applicant's social

Pizza Shuttle, Inc.
1827 N. Farwell
Milwaukee, WI 53202

TODAY'S DATE:

opportunity employer, dedicated to a policy of non-discrimination in employment on
basis including race, creed, color, age, sex, religion or nation origin.

First

Middle Initial Telephone Number

City/State/Zip Code

Social Security Number

BILITY   Check One: ☐ Under 18   ☐ 18 or older

When could you report?

not just preference. (Indicate A.M. or P.M.)   Check one –   ☐ Full

ay	Tuesday	Wednesday	Thursday	Friday	Saturday

o work each week	Minimum	Maximum	Expected weekly salary or hourly pay rate if hired?

Completed   9   10   11   12   /   Grade Average   )

City/State

This job application requests the applicant's Social Security number, so it is not intended to be filled out and submitted over the Internet. Giving out your Social Security number online will make you a potential victim of identity theft.

BEATING JOB FRAUD

People should be careful about giving out personal information when applying for jobs online. Some information—like a Social Security number—should not be needed until after a person gets the job. And then, most employers will let people fill out forms with sensitive personal information and send them through the mail. They understand that sending such information by email can be risky.

security number to get credit cards and buy merchandise.

Auction Fraud

The most common online fraud scheme is auction fraud. More than 35 percent of the complaints the IC3 receives concern auction fraud. In some

Before applying for a job over the Internet, job seekers should check out the company. That way, they know with whom they are dealing. Applicants should try to get the company's address and phone number and then check out the company with the local Better Business Bureau or the Chamber of Commerce. Important to remember: The person seeking employment is not supposed to pay money to land a job. Job hunting does not work that way.

auctions, the seller describes one item and sends an item that is damaged, does not work, or is of lesser quality. The seller refuses to give a refund or replace the item. The second most common complaint (24.9 percent) is that after the auction ends and the buyer pays for the item, the item is never sent to the buyer.

For those who participate in online auctions, it is crucial to deal with a reputable auction site. Before bidding on any auction site, people should learn all they can about the site. Especially important is the site's policy for handling disputes and whether the site stands behind its sellers and buyers. Sometimes customers can leave feedback about a seller. If that is available, bidders should read that feedback before dealing with a particular seller. They should also be familiar with the return policy of the seller and the site.

Don't Be Afraid to Ask

Sometimes buyers have questions about the items up for bid. They should ask any questions of the seller before placing a bid. For instance, a DVD purchased outside the United States may not work in a DVD player made in the United States. Bidders should save all emails connected to their purchase. The same can be said about any financial dealings over the Internet. If a person becomes the victim of a scam, police will need to know details. The correspondence between the buyer and the seller will help police investigate the incident.

People often use a credit card to purchase auction items over the Internet. Before doing this, buyers should learn a little about the auction site—or any business for that matter. Most legitimate auction sites give full information regarding their procedures, payment options, and security. Customers may also email ahead of time and find out about the security measures the site uses to protect personal information and credit card numbers. With the right security safeguards, using a credit card is often a good way to pay. It gives the buyer a chance to refuse a charge if an item never arrives, is damaged, or is not as described in the listing.

Bidders need to be especially careful when making online purchases outside the United States. In this case, they will want to get as much information about the company as possible beforehand. But bidders also must be aware that it is difficult to resolve a problem outside of the United States. Many U.S. laws simply do not apply elsewhere.

No one should let the excitement of making a great deal cloud his or her good judgment. In one recent case reported by the FBI, a scammer in California offered tickets to expensive seating at sporting events through an online auction and never delivered the tickets. He was caught, charged with 12 counts of fraud, and faces up to

The FBI's Fraud Alert checklist gives a rundown of things to be on the lookout for when doing business online. The Bureau encourages people who have paid for an item but never received it, or those who have been victims of auction fraud, to report the incident to the Internet Crime Complaint Center (www.ic3.gov).

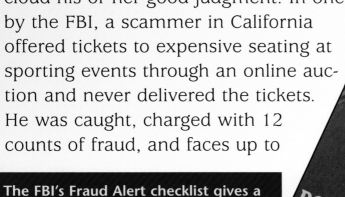

53

20 years in prison. The IC3 reported receiving a number of complaints recently about auto auction fraud. The auctions offer excellent prices on cars, but the bidders never get the cars. Once they win the auction, the bidders are told to wire the money, including shipping fees, to a certain account. Sadly, the car is never delivered. The FBI warns that making major purchases like these over the Internet is always risky, unless the buyer knows the seller personally.

Common-Sense Strategies to Foil Cyber Crooks

Updating a computer operating system helps ensure that it has all the latest technology, including security updates. It is just as important to install and update antivirus software and spyware. People sometimes forget to update these programs regularly. Without this protection, they are leaving themselves open to computer criminals. **Firewall** protection is also recommended. If a computer has a firewall, it should always be on. There is no reason to have a firewall and not use it.

With high-speed Internet connections, most people leave the computer on all the time. They feel it is easier than turning the system off when it is not in use. But this gives cyber criminals unlimited access to the computer. Turning the computer off during long periods of inactivity severs a would-be attacker's connection.

Staying Safe in Cyberspace

It is important to get the word out about what people can do to stay safe in cyberspace. Doing so is not meant to make people afraid to use computers. Rather, it is meant to help them avoid becoming a victim of cyber crime—much as

CYBERETHICS

"Cyberethics." The word may not be familiar, but it just might be one of the most important terms connected with cyberspace.

In the early days of television, the National Association of Broadcasters developed the Seal of Good Practice television code. Today there is a growing need to establish a code of responsible behavior in cyberspace. The FBI and the Department of Justice (DOJ) are using the term "cyberethics" to talk about it. They use the term to teach both children and adults what makes acceptable and legal behavior online.

The Department of Justice and other government agencies are urging schools and parents to teach children about cyberethics. As they do, the adults themselves will learn more about it as well. This will promote the practice of ethical and responsible online behavior across a wide spectrum. The goal is to keep the Internet safe from predators, scam artists, and cyber crooks of all kinds. This will allow the Internet to serve as the powerful information tool it was designed to be.

Many Web sites (including those of the FBI, the DOJ, the American Library Association, and the Federal Trade Commission) offer tips on Internet safety and cyberethics. These sites explain the legal and illegal uses of the Internet and the penalties associated with making the Internet a criminal tool. The DOJ has developed a lesson plan in cyberethics for use in elementary and middle schools. The plan includes guides to help parents explain the basics of cyberethics to children (see http://www.usdoj.gov/criminal/cybercrime/cyberethics.htm#docc).

Cyberethics is crucial for children's safety. It gives them an understanding at an early age about what is ethical and legal behavior online. It helps them learn to act responsibly while using the Internet. But the FBI is hoping this information also will teach young people to spot cyber crime themselves. Once they recognize the crime, they can report it, avoid falling victim to it, and, of course, avoid committing it themselves.

National Cyber Security Awareness Month is observed each October. It calls attention to the battle to keep cyberspace safe for everyone.

Neighborhood Watch programs help residents of a particular neighborhood prevent crime close to home. In a similar way, following common-sense tips such as those offered in this book will help people in the online community steer clear of cyber crooks. Many valuable resources are listed in the section called "Internet Resources" at the back of this book. One of these designed especially for schools and kids is the National Crime Prevention Council. Together with its popular canine crime prevention mascot McGruff, it has launched a national cyber crime prevention program.

FBI special agents are determined to catch cyber criminals. But they are just as determined to prevent cyber crime and cyber terrorism from happening in the first place. To do this, they know they must work with all segments of the cyber community—from individuals to major corporations to foreign countries. As FBI Director Mueller says, "The enemies . . . are at the gates, and we must rely on our agility, our resourcefulness, and our resolve to stop them, together."

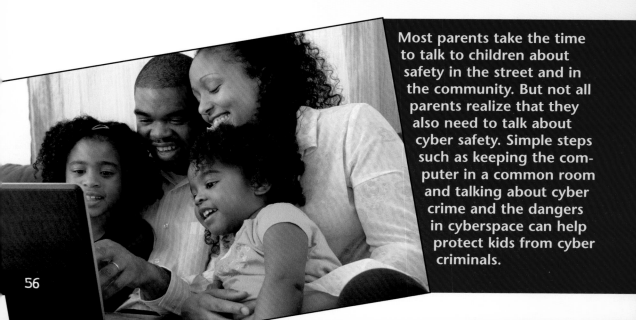

Most parents take the time to talk to children about safety in the street and in the community. But not all parents realize that they also need to talk about cyber safety. Simple steps such as keeping the computer in a common room and talking about cyber crime and the dangers in cyberspace can help protect kids from cyber criminals.

CHRONOLOGY

1996: The FBI establishes InfraGard, a network dedicated to combating and preventing cyber crime. It is started out of the FBI's Cleveland field office.

1998: InfraGard becomes a national effort by 1998.

2000: The Internet Crime Complaint Center (IC3) begins keeping statistics about cyber crime. Since this time, more than one million complaints have been recorded.

2003: In February, President George W. Bush establishes the National Strategy to Secure Cyberspace, the framework to battle cyber crime and protect cyberspace.

2005: The Zotob worm invades and disables computer systems everywhere. The FBI tracks the culprits to Turkey and Morocco and, with the permission of those countries' governments, sends two Cyber Action Teams (CATs) to the source of the worm, where arrests are made.

2005: In the 10-year period from 1996 to 2005, the FBI's Innocent Images National Initiative obtained 4,822 convictions of online child predators.

2006: In September, the FBI hosts a meeting in Washington, D.C., of cyber cops from Canada, New Zealand, Australia, and the United Kingdom. Agents from these countries and the United States form the Strategic Alliance Cyber Crime Working Group, a partnership dedicated to fighting cyber crime on a global level.

2007: The National Cyber Investigative Joint Task Force (NCIJTF) is launched.

2008: The Rochester Institute of Technology conducts a computer use survey of 40,000 adolescents.

GLOSSARY

anonymity—being unnamed or unidentified; the state of keeping one's identity secret.

bot herder—computer hackers who plant software, known as bots, on computers without the owners' knowledge.

brazen—shameless; upfront in doing something wrong.

breach—violation, as of computer security systems.

collaborative—joint, as a cooperative effort between more than one organization.

configured—made up, as in a computer network.

counterparts—people in corresponding or similar positions.

cyber crime—a crime committed in a computer network or by using computer technology.

diabolical—vicious; malicious.

digital forensics—scientific analysis of electronic evidence, as from a computer used in the commission of a crime.

entrepreneur—a person who creates or organizes a business, usually taking on financial risks in the hopes of making a profit.

ferret out—to search out; get to the bottom of something.

firewall—a part of a computer designed to limit unwanted access.

foil—to disrupt; get in the way of.

fraud—using tricks or lies to get another person's money or property.

hacker—someone who uses computers to gain unauthorized access to data, usually data found on someone else's computer.

infrastructure—the basic structures needed for the operation of something. For example, roads, tunnels, mass transportation, buildings, and power supplies are systems that have long been part of a city or region's infrastructure. Today, the components of cyberspace—the computers, software, information networks, and digital technology that help run these systems—are also part of the infrastructure.

intellectual property—a product of the mind or of a creative process, such as an original idea, song, or invention.

intrusions—invasions; disruptions, as of a computer network.

irony—a situation that is completely unexpected and goes against conventional wisdom.

negligent—careless; lax.

obliterated—destroyed.

pedophiles—people who have a sexual interest in young children.

ply—to carry out.

predators—people who victimize others.

restitution—reimbursement, or repayment, for a loss or injury.

robust—strong; forceful.

systemic—systemwide; across an entire system.

trolling—searching for, often with sinister motives.

undaunted—not afraid.

windfall—unexpected good fortune, especially in the form of cash.

wreak havoc—to cause chaos or widespread destruction.

FURTHER READING

Britz, Marie T. *Computer Forensics and Cyber Crime: An Introduction*. Upper Saddle River, NJ: Prentice Hall, 2008.

The FBI: A Centennial History, 1908–2008. Washington, D.C.: U.S. Government Printing Office, 2008.

Grant-Adamson, Andrew. *Cyber Crime*. Broomall, PA: Mason Crest, 2003.

Holden, Henry M. *FBI 100 Years: An Unofficial History*. Minneapolis: Zenith Press, 2008.

Newman, Matthew. *You Have Mail: True Stories of Cybercrime*. New York: Scholastic Library Publishing, 2007.

Warren, Peter. *Cyber Alert: How the World Is Under Attack from a New Form of Crime*. London: Vision Paperbacks, 2005.

INTERNET RESOURCES

http://www.fbi.gov
The official site of the FBI contains the latest information about cyber crime, including statistics on cyber cons, details on recently solved cases, and tips on how to avoid becoming a victim of cyber scams. Look under the "What We Investigate" and "Be Crime Smart" sections to find links to stuff on cyberspace, computers, and the Internet.

http://www.usdoj.gov
This site is a good source of information about the latest cyber crimes and computer intrusions and what the U. S. Department of Justice is doing about it both nationwide and on a global scale. Also offers information on cyber terrorism. Just enter whatever topic you want to read about in the "Search" box.

http://www.ncfta.net
The official Web site of the National Cyber-Forensics and Training Alliance features information about the latest cyber crimes and training methods being used to combat cyber crime and cyber criminals.

http://www.ic3.gov
The Internet Crime Complaint Center's Web site contains annual reports and press releases as well as information on how to report cyber crime and prevention tips.

http://www.nw3c.org
The official Web site of the National White Collar Crime Center has information and up-to-date statistics on cyber crime, as well as white-collar crime, and details on the latest cases and investigative breakthroughs.

http://www.bytecrime.org
The official site for the Take a Bite Out of Cyber Crime campaign, whose mascot is McGruff, the National Crime Prevention Council's crime prevention dog. Just type "cyberspace" or "cyber crime" into the "Search" box for tips on how to avoid becoming a victim of cyber crime and how to stay safe in cyberspace.

http://www.lookstoogoodtobetrue.com
A site dedicated to helping people avoid becoming victims of Internet fraud. Contains information about all the latest scams, as well as older scams, prevention tips, safety tips, and educational materials targeting cyber fraud.

NOTES

Chapter 1

p. 6: "We must act to reduce . . .": George W. Bush, Introductory Letter, The National Strategy to Secure Cyberspace (Washington, D.C.: U.S. Government Printing Office, February 2003).

p. 6: "Securing cyberspace is an . . .": Ibid.

p. 10: "The Internet presents a wealth . . .": Press release, Internet Crime Complaint Center, April 3, 2008. http://www.ic3.gov/media/2008/080403.aspx.

p. 12: "What this report does not show . . .": Ibid.

Chapter 2

p. 18: "Criminals saw the early hackers . . .": "FBI: Cyber-Crime Outlook Is 'Bleak,'" *Wall Street Journal*, September 24, 2007. http://blogs.wsj.com/biztech/2007/09/24/fbi-cyber-crime-outlook-is-bleak/.

p. 22: "We know that [businesses] have . . .": Ibid.

p. 22: "Working side-by-side is not . . .": "Director Mueller to Cyber Professionals: Report Your Hacks!" Headline Archives, FBI Web page, August 12, 2005. http://www.fbi.gov/page2/aug05/infragard081205.htm.

p. 23: "children are most frequently preying . . .": "Cyber Crime Victims 'Often Preyed on by Friends,'" PC Tools, June 19, 2008. www.pctools.com/industry-news/article/cyber_crime_victims_often_preyed_on_by_friends-18646966/.

Chapter 3

p. 28: "All of this makes us . . .": Paula Reed Ward, "FBI Chief Warns of Cyber Crime Dangers," *Pittsburgh Post-Gazette*, November 8, 2007. http://www.post-gazette.com/pg/07312/832168-96.stm.

p. 33: "Cyber-crime is a growing threat . . . .": "Purdue Named Partner in FBI's Cyber Crime Task Force," Press Release, Purdue University, May 19, 2008. http://www.purdue.edu/uns/x/2008a/080519GoldmanTask.html

Chapter 4

p. 42: ""sending a threatening communication . . .": Headline Archives, FBI Web page, October 31, 2007. http://www.fbi.gov/page2/oct07/cybercase103107.html.

p. 44: "The majority of victims are . . .": "Over 1 Million Potential Victims of Botnet Cyber Crime," Press Release, FBI Web page, June 13, 2007. http://www.fbi.gov/pressrel/pressrel07/botnet061307.htm.

p. 45: "An attacker gains control . . .": Ibid.

Chapter 5

p. 46: "The Internet has opened up . . .": Text of speech delivered by Robert S. Mueller III, Director, FBI. Penn State Forum Speaker Series, State College, Pennsylvania, November 6, 2007. http://www.fbi.gov/pressrel/speeches/mueller110607.htm.

p. 56: "the enemies . . . are at the gates, . . .": Ibid.

INDEX

Numbers in **bold italics** refer to captions.

About the Author

Robert Grayson is an award-winning former daily newspaper reporter, and the author of a book of crime victims' services called the *Crime Victim's Aid*. Among the hundreds of articles he has written are pieces on the judicial system, including "Criminal Justice Vs. Victim Justice: A Need to Balance the Scales," published in the *Justice Reporter*. Throughout his journalism career, Robert has written stories on sports, arts and entertainment, business, pets, and profiles. His work has appeared in national and regional publications.